CW01590159

Instant Venice

APA PUBLICATIONS
Part of the Langenscheidt Publishing Group

CONTENTS

Compiled by Jason Mitchell
Photography by Glyn Genin
Additional photography: Ros Miller
Cover: John Heseltine

First Edition 2001

As every effort is made to provide accurate information in this publication, we would appreciate it if readers would call our attention to any errors that may occur by communicating with Apa Publications, PO Box 7910, London SE1 1WE, England. Fax: (44) 20 7403 0290; e-mail: insight@apaguide.demon.co.uk

Distributed in the UK & Ireland by
GeoCenter International Ltd
The Viables Centre, Harrow Way
Basingstoke, Hampshire RG22 4BJ
Fax: (44 1256) 817-988

Distributed in the United States by
Langenscheidt Publishers, Inc.
46–35 54th Road, Maspeth, NY 11378
Tel: (718) 784-0055. Fax: (718) 784-0640

Worldwide distribution enquiries:
APA Publications GmbH & Co. Verlag KG
Singapore Branch, Singapore
38 Joo Koon Road, Singapore 628990
Tel: (65) 865-1600. Fax: (65) 861-6438

Printed in Singapore by
Insight Print Services (Pte) Ltd
38 Joo Koon Road, Singapore 628990
Tel: (65) 865-1600. Fax: (65) 861-6438

www.insightguides.com

THE LADY ON THE SEA

The first fleeting glimpse of Venice from the air is a foretaste of the watery puzzle that awaits below. At low tide, the lagoon reveals an expanse of mud flats, shifting sand banks and brackish marsh; the sunlight momentarily withdraws from the glassy greyish-brown waters, showing the same desolation that failed to daunt early settlers. Yet as the plane circles the lagoon, the sinuous red-brick city floats into view, changing foreboding into fantasy.

Situated mid-way between seductiveness and salaciousness, Venice still relishes its reputation as a place for mistresses and illicit assignations – even if yesterday's unofficial contract of convenience is now swathed in frothy, commercial romance. But the well-deserved reputation for pleasure-seeking should not obscure the Venetians' more refined tastes. Their pronounced aesthetic sense is evident in both art and architecture.

In painting, there is a penchant for colour and sensuality, and for poetic sensibility, rather than for more rational, monumental forms. As for architecture, while the Florentine palazzo is

Above: *Rialto Bridge*

austere and unadorned, the Venetian equivalent is opulent, ostentatious, and decorative almost to the point of gaudiness.

In music, too, the population is remarkably discerning, with a love of composition predating Monteverdi (1567–1643), Vivaldi (1678– 1741) and the foundation of the city's first opera house (1637).

The physical uniqueness of Venice: the mercurial climate, the shimmering light, the slow pace of life, and the watery chimera of the city are reasons enough for loving the place. Only in the *calli* and *campi* of Venice, far from the traffic's roar, can Venetians be themselves, and fully express their open, sociable nature.

The city is split into six *sestieri* (districts), distinct neighbourhoods dotted with parishes. Every parish has its main church, *campo* (square), bar and *alimentari* (food shop) where you can buy *vino sfuso* (draught wine).

Although the distinctiveness of individual parishes is fading, certain districts retain their character. Cannaregio, in particular, is the last bastion for working-class Venetians who have not moved to the mainland. In the remoter parts of Castello, the washing-bedecked alleys are home to children and cats. Around the Rialto lies a surprisingly humble slice of Venetian life, with squalid alleys, but also a popular market – one of the few places where you will only hear Italian or the guttural singsong of Venetian dialect. But throughout Venice, the *campo* or

Above: *coffee in St Mark's Square*

campiello (tiny square) is at the heart of community life. Away from San Marco, Sunday is still spent streaming from church to a *trattoria* for lunch.

Those seeking out Venetian culture are well catered for. The Goldoni Theatre stages plays by the eponymous playwright (1707–93), author of delightful comedies in Venetian dialect. Classical concerts are held in St Mark's as well as in Santo Stefano, San Rocco and La Pietà. Since the destruction of La Fenice, the glorious opera house has been ignominiously relocated to the Palafenice, a tented affair on the island of Tronchetto, also the site of the city car park. And the Film Festival, the Biennale and Carnival are all highlights of the Venetian Social Calendar.

But a trip to Venice would be memorable even if one never stepped indoors: having a *cappuccino* on a terraced cafe, travelling in an open top gondola, or walking in the shimmering sun or the sinister mist of night evokes just as much Venetian spirit as discovering the cultural delights of this magical city.

Above: *a typical Venetian canal*

HISTORICAL HIGHLIGHTS

AD 337 The first recorded settlement around the lagoon.

421 Legendary foundation of Venice on 25 March: Feast Day of St Mark.

568 Mass migrations from the mainland to Venice.

639 The island of Torcello colonised and the cathedral founded.

726 Election of Orso Ipato, the first recorded Doge (Venetian ruler). He rules the lagoon from the now-vanished Heraclea.

814 The population moves to Rivo Alto (Rialto), a more hospitable and easily defended island. First Venetian coins minted. Work begins on the first Doge's Palace.

828 Venetians steal St Mark's body from Alexandria.

834 First Basilica San Marco completed.

1000 Venice controls the Adriatic coast. The Marriage to the Sea ceremony is inaugurated in honour of Doge Pietro Orseolo II's defeat of Dalmatian pirates in the Adriatic.

1104 Foundation of the Arsenale naval complex.

1173 First Rialto Bridge begun.

1202–4 The Fourth Crusade: the Sack of Constantinople and the Venetian conquest of Byzantium provides the springboard for the growth of the Venetian empire.

Above: *San Marco Basilica*

1271–95 Marco Polo's epic journeys to China.
1284 First gold ducats minted in Venice.
1297 Establishment of a patrician autocracy.
1348–9 Plague kills half the population of Venice.
1309 Work begins on present Doge's Palace.
1310 The Council of Ten established to check individual power and monitor security. It gains a sinister reputation thanks to the brutal efficiency of the Venetian secret police.
1355 Doge Faliero (Falier) beheaded for treason against the Venetian Republic.
1373 Jewish community first established in the city.
1453 Constantinople falls to Turks: zenith of Venetian empire.
1508 League of Cambrai unites Europe against Venice. Titian's *Assumption* hung in the Frari church. Birth of Palladio, architect from the Veneto.
1516 Jews confined the Venetian Ghetto.
1519 Birth of Tintoretto, the celebrated Venetian Mannerist painter.

***Above:** gateway to the Arsenale naval complex*

1528 Birth of painter Paolo Veronese.

1577 Palladio designs Il Redentore church.

1580 Birth of baroque architect Longhena.

1630 Venice struck by plague once again.

1669 Loss of Crete – last major Venetian colony – to the Turks.

1693 Birth of Tiepolo, the rococo artist.

1703 Vivaldi made musical director of La Pietà.

1708 An unusually severe winter freezes the lagoon allowing Venetians to walk to the mainland.

1718 Venice surrenders Morea (Peloponnese) to the Turks signalling the loss of the Venetian maritime empire; Venice keeps the Ionian islands and the Dalmatian coast.

1752 Completion of sea walls.

1755 Casanova imprisoned in Doge's Palace for "impiety, imposture and licentiousness.

1757 Birth of Canova, the neoclassical sculptor.

1790 Opening of La Fenice opera house.

1797 The fall of the 1,000-year-old Venetian Republic. Doge Lodovico Manin abdicates. Napoleon grants Venice and its territories to Austria in return for Lombardy.

1800 Papal conclave in Venice elects Pope as France occupies Venice.

1815–66 Venice ceded to Austria under the terms of the Congress of Vienna.

Above: *exhibit in Scuola Grande di San Rocco*

1846 Venice joined to the mainland by rail causeway.
1848 Failed Venetian uprising against the Austrians.
1866 Venice annexed to Kingdom of Italy.
1895 First Biennale art exhibition causes uproar as a result of Giacomo Grosso's erotic work.
1902 The campanile (belltower) in Piazza San Marco collapses.
1931: A road causeway is built to the mainland.
1945 The British liberate the city from Nazi forces.
1960 Construction of the Marco Polo airport.
1966 The worst flood in Venetian history hits the city.
1979 The revival of the Venice Carnival.
1995 Gianni de Michelis, former city mayor, is imprisoned for corruption.
1996 La Fenice burns down. Worst floods and *acqua alta* (high tides) since 1966.
1997 Radicals desiring separation from Italy briefly capture the belltower of St Mark's.
1997–2001 Planned rebuilding of La Fenice.

Above: *La Fenice opera house after the fire*

PEOPLE AND CULTURE

The Actors

The character of the city "is old, conservative and resistant to change. Here in the historic centre we lack the capacity for renewal, or even the numbers required to effect a change." Massimo Cacciari, the philosopher Mayor of Venice, speaks as ponderously and lugubriously as ever.

Certainly, the population is ageing and in decline, with the number of visitors exceeding the resident population by far. Yet the elusive Venetian spirit transcends such truisms, defies the simple arithmetic of the doom-mongers, and refuses to be confined by the straight-jacket of tourism.

In a city defined by the sea, there can be no fortress mentality, only ebb and flow. In short, the slippery lagoon-dwellers retain their distinctiveness, or as much of it as they ever had. One only has to walk the streets to see that the character of the Venetian is as robust as the city's architecture and as sensual as its paintings.

The Artists

Venetian sensibility reflects a shimmering, watery world. The constantly changing lagoon light creates a fluid sense of space, fostering a mood of impermanence, a suspicion of form and an ambiguity absent from landlocked schools of art. The Venetian school embodies a poetic, painterly sensibility at odds with

Above: *taking the gondola by Danieli*

the rational, monumental and sculptural Florentine style. By the same token, Venice turns its back on the classicism and intellectual rigour of the Romans. To the Venetians, colour, light, texture and space were more important than form.

Giovanni Bellini (c1430–1516) was the leading exponent of Renaissance art in Venice. Although his brother, Gentile Bellini (1429–1507), rose to be official state painter, Giovanni ("Giambellino") was the genius, an unworldly painter less concerned with fulfilling a patron's wishes. In later years, he succeeded his brother as state painter and was also buried in the church of Santi Giovanni e Paolo, the resting place of the Doges.

Venice was comparatively slow to absorb Renaissance values but, largely thanks to Bellini, it evolved its own expressive style. He revitalised Venetian painting, infusing his art with light, literally seen as a medium of grace.

Vittorio Carpaccio (c1465–1523/6) is arguably the most Venetian of painters. Unlike Giovanni Bellini, Carpaccio was

***Above:** buying art by the canalside*

more interested in everyday life than in mood. The influence of Flemish art is apparent in his miniaturist precision. While no great master of perspective, he captured the texture of Venetian life and mastered the minutiae without ever losing the unity of the scene.

His paintings offer an enticing vision of Venetian life: canal-sides crowded with onlookers; pinkish-hued porticos and curious casements and chimneys; ceremonial galleys and gondolas; the noble profiles of confraternity worthies; prelates resplendent in damask copes; cocky young blades in red hose and black Venetian caps; ambassadors conforming to strict protocol; cool Venetian ladies at leisure. Carpaccio specialised in pictorial cycles for the Scuole and also painted for the State.

His *Lion of St Mark* in the Doge's Palace is both a symbolic depiction of the might of the Republic and an animated portrayal of the winged beast dominating St Mark's and the Doge's Palace.

Above: *Titian's* The Annunciation

Giorgione (c1478–1510) has been called "the first modern artist" thanks to the subjectivity of his vision. There are tantalisingly few of his paintings in existence and those that remain are resolutely labelled enigmatic. In Venice, he is noted for two works in the Accademia. *La Vecchia* is both a realistic portrait of an elderly woman and a meditation on old age, accompanied by the telling inscription "with time". Poignantly, Giorgione died young, probably of the plague. *The Tempest* is a poetic and puzzling work that conveys a sense of enchantment disturbed by a mysterious inner tension.

Titian (c1487–1576), known as Tiziano Vecellio in Italian, was the polished master of the Venetian High Renaisance style. After Bellini's death, Titian became the undisputed leader of Venetian painting. Indeed, he was the complete Renaissance artist, with ineffable technique, varied subject matter and mastery of different media. His range remains unsurpassed in Western art, encompassing portraits, paintings, mythological poesy, allegories and altarpieces. His style is characterised by a monumentality akin to Roman painting, by bold design, sweeping forms and sensuous modelling.

Allied to this is his expressive style, gorgeous use of colour and the carnal confidence of his nudes. In spite of this enormous scope, he preferred the soft contours of the Venetian school to the sculptural monumentality of the Roman school.

Above: *Titian's tomb, in the Campo dei Frari*

Titian's greatest paintings in Venice are in the Frari, with the revolutionary nature of *The Assumption* vying with the secular opulence of the *Pesaro Altarpiece*. The *Assumption* echoes the vital confusion of life itself, reinforced by the image of mortals being swept up by the spiritual world.

Tintoretto (1518–94) acquired his nickname ("the little dyer") after his father's trade. Vasari, the father of art criticism, described his painting style as "extravagant, unpredictable, fast-working and resolute: the most formidable brain that painting has ever known." Tintoretto's aims were equally immodest and he stated that he wished to "reconcile the drawing of Michelangelo with the colours of Titian." It is not fanciful to call the Scuola Grande di San Rocco Tintoretto's Sistine Chapel. Tintoretto brought a new passion and religious fervour to Venetian painting.

Veronese (1528–88) was nicknamed after his native city of Verona, but his concerns were utterly Venetian. As the art critic John Steer says, "If colour is the most characteristic quality of Venetian art, then the most essentially Venetian artist of his period is Veronese." As a colourist, he was the true successor to Bellini, while in his striving for splendour and decorative detail, his works echoed the Byzantine style. Veronese captured the taste of the times and was chosen to work on the decoration of the Doge's Palace: *The Apotheosis of Venice* is one of his finest mythological scenes. To great acclaim, he created the sumptuous painting in San Sebastiano church, where he is buried.

Above: *Tintoretto's* The Adoration of the Shepherds *(detail)*

Antonio Canal (1697–1768), known as Canaletto, was greatly admired for his limpid landscapes and photographic observations. In Venice, he worked from nature – unusual for the period – creating detailed views *(vedute)* that influenced generations of landscape painters. Yet his early career as a painter of stage-sets meant that a theatrical approach coloured these scenes.

Giambattista Tiepolo (1696–1770) is celebrated for his sublime artifice, heroic style and a virtuosity reminiscent of the Old Masters. Tiepolo was taken under the wing of the Venetian aristocracy: his heroic style, inventiveness and bravura display of skills struck a chord with his patrons, leading to commissions to decorate the finest palaces. Tiepolo's palette consisted of delicate, airy colours to make the space within his pictures shine with an unearthly radiance. This has earned him the epithet of "poet of light".

Yet despite the ethereal settings, his figures have a fleshy, corporeal quality. His was a beguiling and grandiose vision but also one throbbing with sensuality. Tiepolo's triumphal allegories gave visual expression to the autocratic political ideology that dominated the Europe of his day.

***Right:** Doge's Palace, Scala d'Oro*

The Singers

Naturally, Venice maintains a distinguished tradition in "le opera" in this, one of the world's most operatic cities. The leading composers of their day wrote works for Venice, from Rossini and Bellini to Verdi and Wagner. Handel and Scarlatti both conducted their own operas in Venice.

Claudio Monteverdi (1567–1643) is regarded as the founder of Venetian opera. Summoned to Venice after an early musical career at the Mantuan court, he was appointed choirmaster of San Marco and Master of Music for the Republic, remaining in his post for 30 years. He was the traditional successor to **Andrea Gabrieli** (1510– 86) and his nephew **Giovanni Gabrieli** (1557–1612), the early masters of massed choirs and baroque polyphonic music. Monteverdi wrote seven of his operas in Venice, proving his command of musical characterisation.

The Set

Architects call Venice an artificial city: "a city born adult". It was never a blank slate but built from remnants of ruined cities. Venice salvaged Roman bricks from Adriatic villas and recycled arches from churches and palaces in Torcello. Venice raided Byzantium for booty to adorn its noble facades. From marbles to mosaics, the eastern colonies provided precious materials to transform the inhospitable lagoon islands into an imperial capital.

Above: *musicians serenade visitors in St Mark's Square*

Any canal trip shows the vernacular Venetian style is a hybrid. A typical cluster of buildings may include influences from East and West, sport Moorish windows, a Gothic structure, Veneto-Byzantine decoration and Renaissance or baroque flourishes. Craftsmen from Constantinople worked on the oldest buildings, as did Greek mosaicists. To appreciate the early city settlement, there is no substitute for visiting the remote island of Torcello.

Given the Venetian talent for fusion, the emergence of a unique Veneto-Byzantine style was par for the course. The Veneto-Byzantine style (11th–13th century) was an Oriental, flowery form, with ornate capitals and pediments. Slender columns and stilted arches gave way to Moorish design, especially the horseshoe arch and the inflected arch, resembling a quivering flame.

The Byzantine love of voluptuous materials, from inlaid marble to porphyry and jasper, led to facades adorned with paterae, decorative stone or marble plaques, often bearing symbolic foliage and animal motifs: gryphons, eagles, lions, and peacocks

Above: *Rialto Bridge*

symbolising eternal life through baptism, or vine leaves representing the "true vine" of St John's Gospel.

From the 14th century, the intricate floriated Gothic style became common. The Frari is the most glorious of Venetian-Gothic churches. It has a severe facade with a curved crowning and cross-vaulted roof. Santi Giovanni e Paolo, known as Zanipolo, is almost as grand, with a similar cross-vaulted roof. Exposed beams are a feature of many Gothic city churches, with the finest taking the form of ship's keel ceilings, as in Santo Stefano, San Polo and San Giovanni in Bragora.

The end of the 15th century was a golden age for all Venetian art forms, a flowering which was Renaissance Venice. Yet although palaces acquired a classical air, native conservatism prevailed and a hybrid of Venetian Gothic survived well into the 16th century.

The Arsenale, with its crenellations and ceremonial land gate, is considered to be the first flowering of Renaissance architec-

Above: *Grand Canal with La Salute church as a backdrop*

ture. Built in 1460, the land gate leads to the armaments and shipbuilding complex. Other key structures were Antonio da Ponte's Rialto bridge and the Giants' Staircase in the Doge's Palace.

The High Renaissance was led by Jacopo Sansovino (1486–1570), who quickly adapted to the Venetian sensibility despite his Tuscan background and Roman training. In his role as Superintendent of the Works, he had great influence over Venetian architecture. Ca' Grande on the Grand Canal is a magnificent classical triumph. He is responsible for several buildings at San Marco, from the Zecca (Mint) to the Libreria Sansoviniana.

If the Renaissance was the apogée of refinement, baroque Venice belonged to a bold yet less-inspired age. The style is characterised by stone rustication and heavy ornamentation. It revels in exuberant stucco-work and flamboyant friezes, with every surface studded with garlands, cherubs, coats of arms or grotesque masks. The inner courtyard became a grand feature of a palace, with gardens often disappearing. As the prime exponent of Venetian baroque, Baldassare Longhena (1598–1682) created the theatrical church of La Salute, with its grandiose plan indebted to Palladio's Il Redentore.

In both churches and palaces, Longhena was noted for his sense of chiaroscuro (use of light and shadows), in dynamic and dramatic facades heavily charged with rich carving. He is also responsible for breaking the three-part rhythm of the Venetian palace by introducing a continuous sequence of windows.

Right: *Casa dei Tre Oci Giudecca*

Ca' Pesaro has a theatrical inner courtyard and a rusticated Grand Canal facade rich in ornamentation and chiaroscuro effects. Ca' Rezzonico, also designed by Longhena, is more restrained.

The 18th century witnessed a reaction against baroque and a return to Classical values. Grandiose palaces were designed for wealthy *arrivistes*, with stateliness emphasised by monumental staircases. Palazzo Grassi, for example, was based on baroque plans by Longhena but then completed by Massari (1686–1766), an architect who was drawn to the new spirit of the Classical revival. Massari also created the facade of the Gesuati church and his great masterpiece, the church of La Pietà.

The Cooks

For seafood lovers, the cuisine can be memorable, with soft-shell crabs from Murano, plump red mullet, pasta heaped with lobster or black and pungent with cuttlefish ink. Like their southern neighbours the Sicilians, the Venetians absorbed culinary ideas from the Arabs; they also raided Byzantium and, according to the Middle Eastern cookery writer Claudia Roden, translated it into their own simple style.

From the end of the 18th century, French influence meant that Oriental spices were supplanted by Mediterranean herbs. The French brioche was eagerly added to the breakfast repertoire, as was the Belgian waffle and the Turkish *crescente* (literally "a crescent").

Above: *relaxing at a canalside cafe*

The Austrian conquest may have left Venice with a bitter taste in its mouth but it also left the city with an appetite for sweet apple strudel and *krapfen* (doughnuts).

A classic Middle-Eastern inspired dish is *sarde in saor*, tart sardines marinated in the standard Venetian sauce, *saor. Melanzane in saor*, made with aubergines, is the vegetarian version. It is a spicy sauce made with onions, white wine, raisins, vinegar, pine-nuts and olive oil.

Riso (rice), introduced by the Arabs, rather than pasta, is the predominant canvas for a culinary display. Creamy Venetian risotto can be flavoured with spring vegetables, meat, game or fish. *Risi e bisi* ("rice and peas") is a thick soup with ham, celery and onion, the star of rice dishes. A trademark dish is *granseola*, a large crab, boiled and then dressed simply in lemon and oil.

Another staple is *baccalà* (also known as *stoccafisso*) dried salt cod, prepared with milk and herbs, or parmesan and parsley, and served in countless ways, including on toasted bread. In Venice, fish features more often than meat but offal is favoured, particularly in *fegato alla veneziana*, calf's liver sliced into ribbons and cooked with parsley and onion in olive oil.

Pastries, cakes and desserts are a forte, flavoured with exotic spices ever since the Serene Republic first discovered cinnamon and nutmeg.

Above: *a colourful array of produce at Rialto Market*

The Veneto produces a number of superior wines, from the fruity, garnet-red Bardolino to the less prestigious Valpolicella. Soave is the Veneto's best-known white, which comes from some fine vineyards dotted along the eastern shores of Lake Garda.

The Party

Every year the city indulges in a ten-day masked ball, a Lententide "farewell to the flesh". A combination of poseurs and voyeurs come to wallow in the ghostly beauty of Venice as La Serenissima awakes to a whirl of colour, masks and costumes. Venice Carnival is virtual reality for dreamers and insomniacs. Expect to spot a Doge flaunting a drink habit, a libidinous nun locked in an embrace with an 18th-century fop, or Casanova threading the dark canals with a Venetian alley-cat in tow.

Carnival has much to answer for: prices soar and the city has more mask shops than butcher's; fashion shoots and foreign film crews swamp San Marco; cavorting crowds of motley Europeans dress as gondoliers and bosomy courtesans. Amidst air-kissing and cries of "bellissimo", there are displays of pan-European bad taste. These are all travesties of carnival but carnival is a time for travesty. Despite the commercialism, this kitsch masquerade retains its magic. The city exudes a feeling of decadence and faint menace. Carnival unfolds with strangely sinister scenes: cadaverous creatures rowing to the rhythm of the church bells.

***Above:** bundles of goodness in Rialto Market*

The Jewish Ghetto

According to the 1875 Cook's Handbook, "The houses are immensely tall, the streets ridiculously narrow, and a great deal of filth abounds." Thus was the world's oldest Jewish ghetto dismissed. Today, the Ghetto is quiet and unobtrusive, far from the typical tourist attractions. Nothing about the neglected facades of these drab tenements would suggest that until the 17th century this was one of the major Jewish communities in Europe.

Grim though the Ghetto is, it must be seen in the context of the times. Venice was one of the few states to tolerate the Jewish religion: the city was a liberal enclave compared with the brutal regimes of 15th-century Spain or the Ottoman Turks.

Today the local Jewish community numbers 600, with few choosing to live in the former Ghetto. Nonetheless, the Ghetto remains at the heart of Jewish life, with fine synagogues and a cultural centre, a nursery, an old people's home, workshops selling liturgical objects and a kosher bakery.

Above: *bric-a-brac figures for sale*

The City on Celluloid

The city has inspired countless directors, from the Lumière brothers in 1896 to a host of foreign directors a century later. Although art-house films and period dramas predominate, the odd adventure movie provides a change of pace. The James Bond film *Moonraker* (1979) includes a frenzied gondola chase with the agent 007 discovering an enemy hide-out in St Mark's Clocktower. *Indiana Jones and the Last Crusade* (1989) features a crypt full of crusader knights under San Barnaba church. In the French *Le Guignolo* (1980), Jean-Paul Belmondo, playing a daring smuggler, zooms into the famous Hotel Danieli in a motorboat.

Antonioni's masterpiece, *Identification of a Woman* (1982), has scenes set in the misty lagoon and Hotel Gritti. Fellini's *Casanova* (1976) charts the adventures of the Venetian libertine with great aplomb while *Don Giovanni* (1979) has atmospheric scenes of masked figures in the mist.

By contrast, Luchino Visconti's *Senso* (1954) traces a doomed romance in the days of Austrian occupation. While the Italian countess hurries through the gloomy Ghetto Nuovo to meet her Austrian lover, the courtesan heroine (Jeanne Moreau) waits in chic Caffè Lavena on Piazza San Marco. David Lean's *Summertime* (1954) cast Katherine Hepburn as an American who falls into the San Barnaba canal.

The Wings of a Dove (1997), based on the dying heroine in Henry James's classic, makes magnificent use of the palaces along

Above: *part of Visconti's* Senso *was filmed in the Ghetto Nuovo*

the Grand Canal, including the Palazzo Barbaro, where James once lived. However, the undisputed Venetian masterpiece is Visconti's *Death in Venice* (1970), based on Thomas Mann's novel. Dirk Bogarde plays the leading role of the lugubrious composer, von Aschenbach, who mutely adores Tadzio, the Polish golden boy. Visconti wanted "the light of the sirocco, the pale, still, pearl light". The result is exquisite, with an atmosphere of decay conveyed by scenes shot in the early morning light of the Lido. The film is mainly set on the Lido's busy Alberoni beach and in the majestic Hotel des Bains.

Nic Roeg's *Don't Look Now* (1973) is the only other portrayal of the city that seeps into one's bones. Although in thrall to Venice, he captures the faintly menacing mood of the city in winter: "Of course, beauty has its sinister side. For example, one of the strange things about walking in Venice is that you can hear people but don't see them." In this terrifying film, the austere church of San Nicolò dei Mendicoli is an important location.

Above: *the Hotel des Bains, the setting for* Death in Venice

A–Z OF VENICE

The Accademia

As the world's finest collection of Venetian art, the Accademia is the city's most popular gallery. La Carità, a complex of church, convent, cloisters and charitable confraternity houses the collection. Deconsecrated in Napoleonic times, the church became a repository of work created during the Venetian Republic, including paintings saved from suppressed monasteries.

Highlights include 15th-century works by Carpaccio and the Bellini brothers, 16th-century paintings by Giorgione, Titian, Tintoretto and Veronese, and 17th- and 18th-century works by Tiepolo, Guardi and Canaletto *(see artists, page 10).*

The Arsenale

The Arsenale symbolized Venetian maritime might. Founded in 1104, this secretive military and naval complex became Europe's largest medieval shipyard and a powerhouse of industrial planning. The term "Arsenal" derives from the Arabic *darsina'a*, or house of industry, a most suitable description of this Venetian production line.

The Arsenale functioned as a city within a city, bounded by 3 km (2 miles) of walls, with wet and dry docks and ordnance depots and an armaments site. At its height, 16,000 people toiled in the foundries, gunpowder mills and munitions depots, the hemp and sail factories, the ropeworks and grain stores.

Industrial bakeries produced the horribly dry Venetian biscuits that were admirably suited to preservation for consumption on long sea voyages but less acceptable to modern palates. The Arsenale's

Left: *the Arsenale – a city within a city*

industrial caulkers' vats so impressed Dante that he described them in his *Inferno*, making immersion in the bubbling cauldrons of pitch a hellish punishment for corrupt officials.

In its 16th-century heyday, the Arsenale could deliver a fully rigged galley within a day. As a party trick in 1574, the Venetians impressed Henri III of France by producing a seaworthy vessel complete with a 16,000-pound cannon in the time it took him to devour a state banquet.

Basilica di San Marco

John Ruskin called St Mark's "a treasure heap, a confusion of delight". Modelled on Byzantine churches in Constantinople, San Marco transposes the essence of an Oriental basilica to the West. Charles Dickens (1812–70) commented "opium couldn't build such a place... dim with the smoke of incense; costly in treasure of precious stones and metals; glittering through iron bars; holy with the bodies of deceased saints".

Above: *St Mark's Basilica, modelled on Byzantine churches*

The Basilica was consecrated in AD 832, intended as a mausoleum for St Mark's relics and the Doge's ceremonial chapel. In 976 the church burnt down after a riot. The present building's construction began in 1063. Since Venice still recognised the cultural supremacy of Byzantium, the Basilica echoed eastern models.

Behind the altar sits the Pala d'Oro, a superb medieval altarpiece studded with gems and covered in sacred scenes. A gilded frame encloses the panels, encrusted with emeralds, rubies, sapphires and translucent enamels bound by a filigree of gold. The mosaics form a bewildering and beguiling tapestry, an illustrated Bible covering 4,000 square metres.

The Treasury incorporates a 9th-century corner tower from the first Doge's Palace and displays Byzantine gold, silver and glassware. Since this collection began with the Venetian looting of Constantinople, it seems only poetic justice that French plundering should have depleted the treasury. However, much remains, despite a forced sale of jewels and the Napoleonic melting down of *objets d'art*.

The famed Golden Horses of St Mark are also Byzantine booty. The rearing horses stood on top of a triumphal arch in Rome before gracing the hippodrome in Constantinople and finally adorning the facade of San Marco. They are now displayed in the Museo Marciano.

***Right:** the golden ceiling of the Scala d'Oro in the Palazzo Ducale*

The Biennale

The Biennale inhabits the Giardini Pubblici, gardens lined by paths leading to designer pavilions. These permanent pavilions house about 40 countries, with space set aside for international exhibitions. The pastoral nature of the site makes a pleasing contrast to the slick modernism of the exhibits.

Famous architects built a number of the pavilions; notably Josef Hoffman's Austrian pavilion (1934), Carlo Scarpa's Venezuelan pavilion (1954) and Alvar Aalto's Finnish creation (1956). According to art critic Waldemar Januszczak, distortions of national rivalries are alive and well: "The British pavilion stares across at the German"; yet while the British space is classically Palladian, the German building is "one of the few bits of full-blown Nazi architecture to survive outside Germany."

The newest star, James Stirling's Book Pavilion (1994), faces the vast Italian pavilion. Inspired by naval design, this spacious glass and copper structure resembles an overgrown *vaporetto* (water bus). *www.labiennaledivenezia.net/gb/*

Burano Island

This most vibrant of Venetian islands makes a cheery stop en route to Torcello, its polar opposite. Hemingway mocked the islanders for having nothing better to do than make boats and babies. However, Burano is better known as the home of fishermen and lace-sellers. There are few

Above: *La Biennale has slick exhibits from around the world*

cultural sights but atmosphere aplenty. Burano feels a little like an authentic old fishing village, with nets hung out to dry and boxes of crabs blocking the doorways. Burano romantics even portray lace-making as an aesthetic extension of the net-mending tradition.

Fishermen's cottages line Via Galuppi, the main street. The lace shops display the other traditional work of the island, while the *trattorie* is the place for the best crab and squid dishes.

The Scuola dei Merletti, the lace school and museum, inhabits a Gothic palace. Given the difficulties of preserving lace, most samples on display tend to be from the 19th century. This school saved the Burano industry after its decline in the 18th century.

Ironically, the islanders now import Taiwanese lace to boost their scant sales of hand-made lace. Genuine hand-made Burano-point lace is ridiculously expensive: but then, it takes 10 women up to three years to make a single tablecloth, with each woman specialising in a different stitch.

Above: *painted fishermen's houses on Burano Island*

Ca' D'ario Palazzo

Five centuries of scandals, suicides and suspicious deaths have left Venetians wary of this unfortunate canalside palace. Yet it feels secretive rather than sinister. The Gothic palace belonged to Giovanni Dario, a Venetian chancery secretary who negotiated peace with the Turks in 1479. He built this symmetrical Renaissance facade in a jewel-box design, adding the inscription: "to the spirit of the city". The house's history suggests that the spirit is malign.

The curse supposedly started after Dario's daughter died of a broken heart after marrying into the patrician Barbaro family. Although the Barbaro dynasty retained the palace until the 19th century, they suffered scandals and disasters, including the massacre of most of the family during the 17th century.

With Venetians reluctant to buy the palace, an Armenian diamond merchant bought it, and then became bankrupt, dying in penury. After squandering money on restoring Ca' Dario in the 1840s, Rawdon Brown, an Englishman and a friend of the aesthete John Ruskin, committed suicide in the drawing room. In 1936, the melancholic French poet, Henri de Régnier, died shortly after moving in.

More recently, Charles Briggs, a colourful American, held homosexual orgies in the palace and was expelled from the city. In 1979 the jinx supposedly led to the death of Count Giordano

Above: *the accursed Ca' D'ario Palazzo* ***Right:*** *the Ca' d'Oro*

delle Lanze, whose male lover battered him to death with a candlestick. The next owner, a Venetian, became bankrupt and his sister was murdered. The most recent illustrious victim was Raul Gardini, an Italian industrialist, who committed suicide in 1993 after being caught up in the "Zangentopoli" corruption scandals.

Since then, the palace has lain empty. Prospective purchasers may be tempted by the superb interior: Dario's Oriental leanings caused him to add an "Arab kiosk", an enclosed terrace and minaret-style effect. Purchasers may also appreciate the silk-hung drawing room, coffered ceilings, chandeliers of Murano glass and carved columns of Istrian stone.

Ca' d'Oro (The Franchetti Gallery)

One of the loveliest Gothic palaces, this is a landmark building and a sumptuous version of a Venetian palace. Originally picked out in gold, the friezes of interlaced foliage and mythological beasts on the facade led to its popular name, "the Palace of Gold".

The Ca' d'Oro houses the Franchetti Gallery, arguably the most appealing city art museum. Its idiosyncratic collection reflects the refined taste of the owner. The coffered ceilings and fine marble floors make a splendid showcase for the medieval and Renaissance exhibits. Highlights of the collection include a delightful *Annunciation* by Carpaccio, Guardi's views of Venice and Titian's *Venus*. Andrea Mantegna's *St Sebastian*, the most poignant of his paintings, was Franchetti's favourite work. Yet the minor Venetian works give the greatest pleasure, ranging from the 12th-century sculptures of interlaced peacocks to the poetic Byzantine-style paintings executed by Vivarini.

Ca' Pesaro (The Museum of Oriental Art and the Museum of Modern Art)

The recently restored Grand Canal facade of the Ca' Pesaro offers a play of chiaroscuro (light and dark) effects created by recessed windows and sharply delineated cornices. The palace now serves as home to the Museum of Oriental Art and to the Museum of Modern Art.

The eclectic 19th-century collection assembled by the Count di Bardi on his travels to the Far East contains Japanese art

Above: *Titian's* The Madonna *is housed in Ca' Pesaro*

of the Edo period (1614–1868) and Oriental decorative works.

The Museum of Modern Art devotes its first floor to temporary exhibitions, with sculpture displayed in the courtyard. The rotating permanent collection is shown on the second floor and includes works by Klimt and Chagall, Klee, Kandinsky, Matisse, Roualt and Morandi.

Ca' Rezzonico (The Museum of 18th-Century Life)

Henry James likened this bold building to "a rearing sea-horse" because of its upward-thrusting cornices. Longhena designed this Baroque masterpiece, probably the most famous palace in the city and one of the few on the Grand Canal open to the public. The poet Robert Browning (1812–89) died in this palace. A wall in the palace bears words taken from Browning's epitaph: "Open my heart and you will see /Graved inside of it Italy".

Ca' Rezzonico houses the Museum of 18th-Century Life (Museo del Settecento Veneziano). The opulent building makes a suitable showcase for Tiepolo's trompe l'oeil ceilings and Guardi's 18th-century genre paintings. The magnificent interior is boldly restored, daringly frescoed and richly embellished with glittering chandeliers and period pieces. The *Sala dell'Allegoria Nuziale* (1758) is a homage to Tiepolo. The frescoed ceiling depicts a nuptial allegory in the *Marriage of Ludovico Rezzonico* with careering horses tumbling through the

Right: *statue in the courtyard of Ca' Rezzonico*

billowing heavens accompanied by angels and cherubs. Elsewhere Tiepolo frescoes depict *Nobility and Virtue* and *Fortitude and Wisdom*. Guardi's Ridotto (1748) shows masked gamblers and revellers in the state casino. His *Nuns' Parlour* (1768) depicts the spirited and worldly nuns whose reputation for lasciviousness made Venetian convents a byword for dissolute living.

Many of Longhi's superior salon pictures, such as *Rhinoceros Show,* show patrician Venice at play. The museum also displays one of the few works by Canaletto in Venice: his *View of Rio dei Mendicanti* (1725).

Campo San Polo

Situated just across the canal of the same name, the Campo San Polo is the heart of a picturesque district. After San Marco, it is the largest Venetian square and one of the most appealing. Today it is a popular venue for film screenings and carnival balls. At different times of the day, the square becomes an impromptu

Above: *the Campo San Polo in the heart of a picturesque district*

football pitch or mother-and-toddlers' meeting place; in the evening, students gather on the benches or meet at the neighbourhood *birreria* in order to listen the latest gossip while enjoying a cool beer.

Campo Santa Margherita

This is the liveliest square in Dorsoduro and the archetypal Venetian meeting place; from Campo Santa Margherita the splendours of the Grand Canal beckon. Neighbourhood shops are set amid homely yet scruffy palaces. Just above several fish stalls lies an ancient stone sign prescribing the minimum size of fish permitted.

A slice of Venetian life can be seen browsing in the antiquarian print shop, discount bookshop or alternative pharmacy. The locals refill dubious countainers at the rustic wine shop while students prefer the friendly bars.

Campo Santi Giovanni e Paolo

Familiarly knows as Zanipolo, this is one of the most monumental squares in Venice. Campo Santi Giovanni e Paolo encloses the great Gothic church of the same name and Renaissance confraternity as well as the finest equestrian statue in northern Italy.

Santi Giovanni e Paolo is the city's most authentic Gothic church. The Gothic pinnacles can be seen from both banks of the Grand Canal, with the roofline displaying statues of the Domini-

Above: *fine equestrian statue of Colleoni, Santi Giovanni e Paolo square*

can saints. The church is conisidered the Pantheon of Venice honouring illustrious leaders from admirals and noblemen to the occasional state artist, notably Bellini. Above all, this was the last resting place of the Doges, with the pomp of state funerals matched by magnificent monuments to 25 Doges.

I Carmini

Home of the Scuola Grande dei Carmini and headquarters of the Carmelite confraternity, the uninspired facade of I Carmini, built by Longhena, conceals a lavishly frescoed 18th-century interior with a monumental twin staircase, complete with barrel-vaulted ceilings encrusted with stuccoes – a splendid showcase to Tiepolo. He also decorated the Salone. Since the wealthy order prospered during the Counter Reformation, with the cult of Mary acting as a counterweight to Protestantism, the Carmelites could afford to summon the services of the greatest rococo painter.

Above: *Tiepolo's lavishly decorated interior of I Carmini*

Tiepolo repaid their confidence with a series of sensuous masterpieces, a floating world of pale skies and illusionistic effects.

Frari

Officially known as Santa Maria Gloriosa dei Frari, this is the largest and greatest of all the Venetian Gothic churches. The hulking Franciscan complex, founded in the 13th century, was rebuilt in the 14th and 15th centuries. The adjoining monastic cloisters house the state archives and 1,000 years of Venetian history.

Giudecca Island

Giudecca contradicts itself more than most Venetian islands, housing the city's most luxurious hotel and one of its most deprived districts. Il Redentore lures most visitors to the island.

Built in thanks for the end of the 1576 plague, the church hosts Venice's most beguiling summer festival *(see page 76)*. The subtle facade rests on a rusticated pediment, with a sweeping flight of steps echoing the style of a gracious Palladian country villa.

From the church, Ramo della Croce leads to the exotic Garden of Eden, named after the Englishman who created it. The Hotel Cipriani, set on the eastern spit of the island, enjoys sweeping views over the lagoon, especially from the summer terrace.

Above: *statue of Christ, Il Redentore church on Giudecca Island*

The Guggenheim Museum

The Palazzo Venier, a white, truncated structure also known as *Nonfinito* (unfinished), houses the Guggenheim Foundation, named after the American millionairess, art collector and benefactor, Peggy Guggenheim (1898–1979), who lived in Venice from 1949 until her death.

This popular collection displays work by such names as Chagall, Dali, Klee, Braque, Giacometti, Kandinsky, Bacon and Sutherland and represents most major movements. Highlights include De Chirico's *Red Tower*, Brancusi's *Bird in Space*, Magritte's *Empire of Light* and Pollock's *Alchemy*.

Sculptures fill the gardens including works by Henry Moore and Marino Marini. (Curiously, the watergates are often closed to conceal the provocative erection sported by the rider in Marini's *Angel of the Citadel*.) *www.guggenheim.org/venice*

Grand Canal

In Venice "the simplest social coming and going assumes at the same time the form and charm of a visit to a museum and a trip to the sea". Marcel Proust captures the entertaining yet educational aspect of a trip along the Grand Canal. Known affectionately as

Above: *the Grand Canal offers a feast for the senses*

the "Canalazzo" (Little Canal), the canal follows the course of an ancient river bed. Nearly 4 km (2½ miles) long and up to 70 metres (230 ft) wide, the surprisingly shallow highway flows under three bridges and past ten churches while over 200 palaces line its sides. This great waterway sweeps through the six city districts *(sestieri)*, with switchbacks providing changing vistas of palaces and warehouses, markets and merchant clubs, courts, prisons and even the city casino.

Once a waterway for merchant vessels and great galleys, the canal now welcomes simpler craft, from gondolas to garbage barges. However, the palaces remain a testament to the city's imperial past. Yet the sea is a great leveller, with low tide revealing the slimy underpinnings of the noblest palace. Several of the grandest art collections border the canal, notably the Accademia (Venetian art of all periods), the Guggenheim (modern art), the

Above: *benefactor of the museum of the same name, Peggy Guggenheim*

Ca'd'Oro (medieval and Renaissance art), the Ca' Rezzonico (18th-century art) and Ca' Pesaro (Oriental and modern art).

The charm of these palaces lies in their variety. As Henry James remarked: "The fairest palaces are often cheek-by-jowl with the foulest, and there are few, alas, so fair as to have been completely protected by their beauty." As well as providing a cavalcade of Venetian pageantry, the Canal offers a slice of local life. Architecturally, the Grand Canal is a feast for the senses.

Harry's Bar

On the basis that Harry's Bar is the best bar in the best city in the world, the famed Bellini cocktail is cheap at any price. The lure of classic cocktails and a good gossip have drawn prominent personalities, from Winston Churchill and Charlie Chaplin to Bogart and Bacall, Fellini and Mastroianni, Frank Sinatra and Madonna.

Ernest Hemingway, footloose in Venice, always found inspiration or oblivion in his favourite bar. As a macho man in a macho bar, he slugged the Montgomery, a martini made with 15 measures of gin to one of vermouth, the same potent ratio of troops to enemy employed by the military strategist.

Sketches of famous guests appear in a book dedicated to the founder. Gore Vidal wrote that, since the closure of the American Consulate in the 1970s, "Harry's Bar is sometimes the only place for Americans in acute distress to go to for comfort and advice."

Above: *Harry's Bar has drawn many prominent personalities*

Jewish Ghetto

Despite its name, Campo del Ghetto Nuovo (New Ghetto Square) stands at the heart of the world's oldest ghetto, a fortified island created in 1516. This moated *campo* contains evocative testaments to the deportation of Jews to the death camps in the form of memorial plaques on several of the buildings around the irregularly shaped square. Three of Venice's five remaining synagogues are set around the square, as unobtrusive as the Ghetto itself.

Although hidden behind nondescript facades, the synagogues reveal lavish interiors, often with a Levantine feel. Builders used gilt and stucco rather than marble, a material forbidden to Jews by the Venetians. The synagogues, known as *schole*, date from 1528 and served as Jewish counterparts to the Venetian *scuole*.

The hinges of the former Ghetto gates can be seen on Sottoportego Ghetto Nuovo, with the overall effect often likened to a drawbridge leading to a mysterious world. Beyond the spacious square and bridge lies the Ghetto Vecchio (Old Ghetto), an overspill ghetto created in 1541, with two more synagogues. The Schola Spagnola, designed for Spanish and Portuguese Jews, built in 1538, gained a baroque facade attributed to Longhena. An oval *matroneum*, or women's gallery, rather reminiscent of

***Right:** detail from the Jewish Ghetto*

the grand circles of Venetian theatres, graces the hall. *www.doge.it/ghetto*

La Pieta

The Ospedale della Pieta was the most famous of the *Ospedali* (institutions combining the roles of orphanage and musical conservatory). The church was the backdrop for concerts given by the choir of orphan girls under Vivaldi's tutelage. It was superbly remodelled by Massari in the 18th-century and transformed into the city's leading concert hall. The magnificent gold and white interior is crowned by Tiepolo's *The Triumph of Faith* (1775).

The Lido

This long strip of land, sandwiched between the city of Venice and the waters of the Adriatic, belongs neither to Venice nor the mainland. In spirit, it is a place apart, not quite a traditional

Above: *the Tempo Votivo at the Lido*

summer resort nor a residential suburb. In this faded fantasy, Neo-Gothic piles vie with Art Nouveau villas and a mock-Moorish castle.

The Lido is home to several of the city's most elegant hotels, including the Grand Hotel des Bains. Thomas Mann's stay in this ecletic Edwardian palace helped inspire *Death in Venice*.

In the Romantic era, Byron and Shelley raced on horseback along the empty sands, but the advent of sea-bathing in the 1840s brought the fashionable elite and the world in its wake. The island became the world's first lido, spawning a rash of brash or glitzy imitators across the globe. Ruskin railed against the crowds of uncouth smokers who filled "his" steamers: the populace "smokes and spits up and down the piazzetta all day, and gets itself dragged by a screaming kettle to the Lido next morning to sea-bathe itself into capacity for more tobacco."

Nuovo Cimitero Israelitico, the Jewish cemetery, dates back to 1386, and on the lagoon shore stands San Nicolò, a church and Benedictine monastery.

Mercerie

Named after the haberdashers' shops that once lined the route, this shadowy maze of alleys run between the Rialto and San Marco. Today, the engaging bazaar sells such traditional souvenirs as marbled paper, Murano glass and carnival masks, leather goods and hand-crafted jewellery.

***Right:** the labyrinthine Mercerie*

Murano Island

"The most curmudgeonly of the Venetian communities, where it always feels like early closing day," denounced writer Jan Morris. In summer, Murano can pass for a smaller version of Venice but it can be very bleak in winter, with scruffiness and commercialism outweighing picturesque charm. Visitors come for the glass-making, although an impressive Byzantine church and a cluster of bars also add to Murano's appeal.

Murano glass is an acquired taste, which many lifelong Venice fans fail to acquire. While few visitors would turn down an antique Murano mirror, modern Murano glass errs on the side of virtuosity and garishness rather than refinement and elegance.

However, the skill of the glass-blowers makes an impressive display. The quayside opens onto Fondamenta dei Vetrai, the heart of the glass-making district. The show-rooms along the quayside offer opportunities to admire the glass-blowers' skills. Museo Vetrario, the Glass Museum, occupies the imposing Palazzo Giustinian, a Gothic palace remodelled in the style of the 17th century.

Santi Maria e Donato is the finest church on Murano, despite a mis-

***Above:** busy canalside on Murano Island, famed for its glassworks*

guided 19th-century restoration. Founded in the 7th century, blind arches and loggias leaning over the canal decorate the 12th-century apses extending from its Gothic ship's keel ceiling, Greek marble columns and Veneto-Byzantine capitals. A luminous Byzantine-style mosaic of the Madonna and Child, rivalled by a charming altarpiece by Paolo Veneziano (c1310) dominates the apse. The patterned mosaic floor, depicting interlaced foliage and allegorical animals, highlights the trip.

Another church, the Gothic San Pietro Martire has a Renaissance portal and a subtle altarpiece by Bellini, *The Madonna, Doge Barbarigo and Saints* (1488).

Museo Correr

Housed in the Procuratie Nuove, the Museo Correr (the Museum of Venetian Civilisation) faces the basilica on the far side of Piazza San Marco. The Neo-Classical rooms make a fine setting for Canova's sculptures. The first section romps through Venetian history, illustrated by representations of the Lion of St Mark, paintings of festivities and examples of ceremonial costume. The final historical section covers the troubled times from the fall of the Republic to French and Austrian domination and the Risorgimento (Revival).

The chronological display of the picture gallery focuses on Venetian art from the 13th to the 16th century. Highlights include

Above: *enjoying the art on show at the Museo Correr*

Byzantine-influenced works by Paolo Veneziano and Bartolomeo Vivarini and paintings by Giovanni Bellini, especially the poignant *Pietà*. When in Venice, much like the *Mon*[illegible]*a* in Paris, you must see Carpaccio's *Two Venetian Ladie*[illegible] [illegible]507), depicted in a pleasure garden, surrounded by birds and dogs.

Museo Navale

Given the tantalising elusiveness of the Arsenale, only in the Naval Museum can you fully appreciate the greatness of maritime Venice. Before its present incarnation, the 16th-century building was used as a naval granary and biscuit warehouse. The Austrians created the collection from those few remnants to survive French depredations.

Apart from naval maps, nautical instruments, uniforms and insignia, the collection includes a range of weaponry, from 17th-

***Above:** view of the Naval Museum and Arsenale*

century breech-loaders to heavy cannons and World War II torpedoes. The specifically Venetian antiquarian maps depict the development of the Arsenale and the lagoon defences, while scenes of naval battles and models of fortresses around the Mediterranean illustrate Venice's naval supremacy.

Models on display range from early Egyptian and Phoenician craft to Greek triremes and a Venetian galley. Gondolas naturally play a prominent role, including examples of boats built with a felze, the wooden cabin that protected passengers from prying eyes and winter weather. One highlight is a scale model of the last Bucintoro, the legendary state barge.

Palazzo Contarini del Bovolo

Concealed in a maze of alleys, this late Gothic Palace (dating from 1499) is celebrated for its romatinc arcaded staircase. *Bovolo*, meaning sail-shell in Venetian dialect, well describes the delightful spiral staircase that is linked to loggias of brick and smooth white stone.

Palazzo Ducale (Doge's Palace)

The Palazzo Ducale (Doge's Palace) vies with San Marco for visitor's attention and plaudits. The seat of the Venetian government from the 9th century until the fall of the Republic

Above: *the delightful Bovolo staircase*

in 1797, it acted as the nerve centre of the Republic, containing administrative offices and armouries, council chambers and chancellery, courtrooms and dungeons.

The Palace symbolised political stability and independence, testified to Venetian supremacy and served as a glorious showcase of art, sculpture and craftsmanship. Yet a shadowy side of the palace existed: a secretive machine staffed by state inquisitors, spies and torturers-in-residence.

Although often considered the symbol of Gothic Venice, the Palace has two of the finest Gothic facades in existence, a vision of rosy Verona marble supported by delicate Istrian stone arcades. Inside, the Giants' Stairway, built in 1486, represents the flowering of Renaissance Venice. Doges were crowned with a ceremonial jewel-encrusted cap at the top of the stairs.

Another famous stairwell, the Scala d'Oro, designed by Sansovino in 1555, is a ceremonial staircase linking the piano nobile with the upper floors. The glittering, gilded setting is a prelude to the superb state rooms, intended to overawe visiting dignitaries.

The rooms reveal the inner workings of the Serene Republic, from the voting procedures to the courts of law. Tintoretto's mythological scenes lavishly decorate the Collegiate rooms. The Sala del Consiglio dei Dieci (the chamber of the feared Council of Ten) has a ceiling decorated by Veronese. The Sala del Maggior Consiglio (the Grand Council Chamber) highlights the

*Doge's Palace interior detail (**above**) and facade (**right**)*

tour with coffered ceilings, paintings and embossed surfaces. Domenico and Jacopo Tintoretto's *Paradise* covers an entire wall. Veronese captured the taste of the times with *Apotheosis of Venice* and a frieze running around the upper walls featuring the first 76 Doges.

If you have even the slightest smattering of Italian, follow the Secret Itinerary (Itinerari Segreti), an exploration of the "shadow-palace": its maze of alleys, secret passageways, and general air of murk and mystery.

En route, one sees the state inquisitors' rooms, torture chamber and prisons, including the famous *Pozzi*, basement cells. Casanova made his daring escape in 1755 from the stifling *Piombi* or Leads, under the eaves of the Palace.

Palazo Grassi

Longhena designed this imposing patrician palace and model of Neo-Classical architecture; Massari completed the palace with due regard to the correct Classical orders. The palace belonged to a patrician family who died out in the 19th century. Now

Fiat use it as a showcase for international exhibitions and the interior has been stunningly converted into an art gallery whose temporary exhibitions compete with the best in the world.

Palazzo Labia

A splendidly restored palace, with the ballroom ceilings frescoed by Tiepolo. Now the headquarters of RAI, the state broadcasting network, the former owners were the noble Labia family, renowned for their extravagance. Once, after a rumbustuous banquet, guests theatrically hurled the gold plates and cutlery into the canal as the host cried out: "Whether I have them or not, I'll always be a Labia". The occasion for this extravagant pun had been planned in advance, with precautionary nets placed in the water to catch the precious heirlooms so they could be salvaged once the party was over. The superb decorations and Tiepolo frescoes can be visited by appointment.

Above: *San Geremia Church on the Palazzo Labia*

Piazza San Marco

Napoleon dubbed Piazza San Marco "the finest drawing room in Europe". Gentile Bellini's *Precession in Piazza San Marco* (1496) is the most reproduced view of Venice, a grand hierarchical affair of prelates and senators outside the Basilica. Yet unlike many official city squares, St Mark's belongs to the citizens as well as visitors.

Venetians themselves will drink at the grand cafes. Some may attend Sunday Mass at the Basilica or even dance at the open-air Carnival. But for most of the day, St Mark's belongs to the pigeons, the crowds and the souvenir-sellers; only in early evening does it revert to some semblance of solitude.

Ponte dei Sospiri (Bridge of Sighs)

The most famous bridge in Venice, the Bridge of Sighs crosses the canal to the "new" prisons, providing a link between the Doge's Palace, courtrooms and cells, allowing interrogators to slip back and forth. Built between 1595 and 1600, this covered stone bridge acquired its legendary name after the lamentation of prisoners as they confronted their inquisitors. In reality, by the standards of the day, the prisons were relatively comfortable.

The new prisons, designed to hold the overspill from the "old" prisons in the Doge's Palace, occupy a sober, Classical building. The old prisons, from which Casanova made his dramatic escape,

***Above:** the Bridge of Sighs, named after the lamentation of prisoners*

were known as *I Piombi* (the Leads), because they were built right under the lead roofs of the Palace. The bridge marks the beginning of Riva degli Schiavoni, the best-known stretch of Venetian waterfront.

Rialto

"What's new on the Rialto?" Antonio cried in Shakespeare's *The Merchant of Venice*. Gossip remains a popular Venetian pastime in this curiously provincial city and the Rialto, with its market and mass of tiny bars, is still a talking shop. The Rialto embraces the district curved around the middle bend of the Grand Canal. The Rialto is often described as "Venice's kitchen, office and back parlour".

Venice's liberal laws and an entrepreneurial culture helped the Rialto become a cosmopolitan centre, a home to a mixture of races and a babble of tongues. Here, northern Italian grain dealers and Flemish wool merchants rubbed shoulders with Jewish money-lenders, Arab spice traders and German metal traders, as well as with Florentine and Lombard cloth merchants.

The Rialto Bridge traditionally divides the city into two, with the right bank, the San Marco side, known as the *Rialto di quà* (this side) and the left bank known as the *Rialto di là* (that side). The Rialto Bridge, with shops selling shoes, silk scarves and jewellery, spans the Grand Canal with a strong elegantly curved arch of marble.

Above: *da Ponte's Rialto Bridge*

Antonio da Ponte designed this new bridge in 1588–91 following the collapse of the previous one. Tradition has it that the greatest architects of the day, including Michelangelo and Palladio, competed for the commission but the aptly named da Ponte won. From the bridge one can admire the majestic sweep of palaces and warehouses swinging away to la Volta del Canal.

Riva degli Shiavoni

Now bustling with tourists and souvenir sellers, this sweeping quayside once thronged with slave-dealers and merchants. Its name refers either to slaves or Slavs, who were often synonymous in Venetian minds. Certainly, the term came to embrace the Dalmatian merchants from Schiavonia, modern-day Croatia, who settled in Venice in great numbers during the 15th century. The quayside was widened and paved in 1782 and has been a popular Venetian promenade ever since.

La Salute Basilica

The baroque basilica of La Salute, a Venetian landmark guarding the entrance to the Grand Canal dominates the city's *sestieri* of Eastern Dorsoduro. Dedicated to Santa Maria della Salute (Our Lady of Good Health), Longhena designed the church as a thank-you for delivery from the plague in 1630. The great

Right: *Riva degli Shiavoni*

baroque architect wished it to be "strange, worthy and beautiful". Henry James's celebrated conceit springs to mind: "like some great lady on the threshold of her salon. She is more ample and serene… with her domes and scrolls, her scalloped buttresses and statues forming a pompous crown, and her wide steps disposed on the ground like the train of a robe".

Begun in 1631, the church took 50 years to complete. The octagonal structure alludes to the symbolic eight-pointed Marian star while the theatrically raised high altar evokes the Virgin's rescue of Venice. The major works of art include Tintoretto's *Wedding at Cana*, paintings by Titian in the sacristy, and a small Byzantine *Madonna*.

San Francesco del Deserto

Visitors must hire a *sandolo*, a Venetian rowing boat to reach this Franciscan island. Legend has it St Francis visited the island on his return from the Holy Land, symbolised by a tree that supposedly sprouted from the saint's staff. A Franciscan community was certainly established here by the 13th century.

A friar takes visitors round the original cloisters and modest 15th-century church. The monastery exudes an air of self-sufficiency, from the serene friars to the well-tended vegetable gardens. A contemplative mood is induced by the lofty cypresses and emblematic Franciscan paintings.

San Giacomo dell'Orio

Although slightly off the beaten track, this charming parish church conveys an inviting Romanesque atmosphere lit by diffuse light. Although founded in the 9th century, the church building spans many centuries. Architectural eclecticism is apparent in the Veneto-Byzantine belltower and columns, wooden Gothic arches, Renaissance apses and the Gothic ship's keel roof.

The finest artworks are a rare 14th-century wooden Tuscan crucifix and, in the New Sacristy, a Veronese ceiling.

San Giorgio Maggiore Island

This majestic monastery island appears suspended in the inner lagoon when seen from afar. The belltower modelled on St Mark's, together with the baroque beacon of La Salute, guard the inner harbour of Venice. San Giorgio is a hallowed spot, with its famous Benedictine monastery, and the absence of bars and commercial distractions allows San Giorgio to retain its secluded air.

The medieval monastery, though remodelled in the late 15th and early 16th centuries, owes its classical grace to Palladio.

Left: *La Salute basilica, San Giorgio* ***Above:*** *San Giorgio Maggiore basilica*

Today, the Benedictines remain the sole island residents, enhancing the mood of spiritual seclusion.

San Giorgio Maggiore is undoubtedly the finest monastic church in the lagoon. Here Palladio shows his mastery of the classical idiom. The facade consists of two overlapping temple fronts, with a central portico. A lift whisks visitors to the top of the belltower for fabulous views over the city, whatever the weather. If the lift attendant is not too busy, he may be persuaded to unlock the Sala del Conclave, where the conclave met to elect Pope Pius VII in 1800 while Rome was occupied by French troops. Although it is now used as a private music room by the monks, members of the public can occasionally attend classical concerts here, as well as performances of Gregorian chant in the church.

The Fondazione Cini occupies much of the great Benedictine complex. Count Vittorio Cini (1884–1977) bequeathed his home to the city and created the foundation as a memorial to his son who died in a flying accident. The centre funds restoration projects and conventions and stages major exhibitions.

Other highlights include the huge Renaissance dormitory and the cross-vaulted Palladian refectory. More impressive still are the Renaissance Cloister of the Laurels *(Chiostro degli*

Above: *interior of San Giorgio Maggiore*

Allori) and the Palladian Cloister of the Cypresses *(Chiostro dei Cipressi)*. Palladio also designed the ceremonial guest quarters overlooking the lagoon. The sumptuous setting is more reminiscent of a palace courtyard than of a cloistered retreat. The Palladian cloisters lead to the monastic gardens and the Teatro Verde, the open-air theatre; this pastoral setting provides an atmospheric stage set for occasional summer concerts.

San Giorgio degli Schiavoni

Founders intended the *scuola* to protect the interests of Slavs from Dalmatia (Schiavonia), the first Venetian colony. On its completion in 1501, the confraternity commissioned a painting cycle in honour of the Dalmatian patron saints, St George, St Tryphon and St Jerome. As the foremost painter of cycles, they chose Carpaccio to decorate the upper gallery but, after the *scuola* was rebuilt in 1551, his masterpieces were moved downstairs.

Despite remodelling, the *scuola* retains its authentic atmosphere and has the only Venetian pictorial cycle still in the building for which it was painted.

San Lazzaro Island

San Lazzaro degli Armeni, an island off the Lido, is one of the most intriguing monasteries in the lagoon, distinguished by its onion-shaped cupola. The island is a scholarly centre for Armenian

Above: *Scuola di San Giorgio degli Schiavoni facade*

culture and supported by the 8-million strong Armenian diaspora. The setting is idyllic, with the church and cloisters surrounded by orchards and strolling peacocks. The remodelled Romanesque church is decorated with starry mosaics, the air laden with incense.

The 18th-century refectory is where the monks and seminarians eat in silence while the Scriptures are intoned in Classical Armenian. The picture gallery and public rooms contain fine Venetian and Armenian paintings, including a work by Tiepolo.

San Michele Island

San Michele, site of the city cemetery is often appropriately swathed in mist. When seen from afar it floats as ethereally as a city in the afterlife. The quayside and adjoining alleys are devoted to the business of death: monumental masons vie with funeral florists. From the shore, one's eye is drawn to the contrast between the solemn cypress trees and the high rose-coloured brick walls.

***Above:** the cloister of San Michele church*

Just by the landing-stage lies San Michele in Isola, a cool, austere Renaissance church by Coducci. As the first church faced in blanched white Istrian stone, San Michele set a building trend throughout the Veneto. Famous foreigners are allowed to rest in peace but more modest souls are evicted after 10 years.

The rambling cemetery is stacked with simple memorials or domed family mausoleums awaiting further members. Here lie the tombs of several Dogal families, obscure diplomats, and the victims of the plague. The grounds are studded with grotesque statuary encompassing the grandiose and monumental, the cute and the kitsch.

In the eastern corner is the Protestant *(Evangelisti)* section, containing the grave of American poet Ezra Pound (1885–1972). Untended and overgrown, this is also the last resting place of obscure Swiss, German and British seamen. In the *Greci* or Orthodox section lie the tombs of composer Igor Stravinsky (1882–1971) and ballet impresario Diaghilev (1872–1929) along with the tombs of long-forgotten Russian and Greek aristocrats.

Venetian nurse Livio Nardo has a sunny relationship with San Michele and says of it: "It's the most cheerful cemetery in the world, as cemeteries go. You've got good company there – Stravinsky and Ezra Pound. We get tourists committing suicide in Venice just so they can be buried there."

Right: *San Michele Cemetery graves*

San Nicolo dei Mendicoli

The most remote waterside church in western Dorsoduro, San Nicolo dei Mendicoli is set in a dilapidated district. This former fishermen's and artisans' church is surprisingly sumptuous: it presents a squat Romanesque belltower and a bare brick facade lit by mullioned windows.

The church is one of the oldest in Venice, founded in the 7th century but remodeled between the 12th and 14th centuries. The interior is embellished with Renaissance panelling, gilded statues and school of Veronese paintings.

San Pietro di Castello

A wooden bridge leads to the island of San Pietro, the site of the original castle *(castello)* that gave its name to the district. San Pietro di Castello rests on ancient foundations but is essentially Palladian, topped by a central dome.

From the founding of Venice until 1807, the church served as the city cathedral, with the title only passing to St Mark's after the demise of the Republic. The interior contains a late work by Veronese and the distinctive Throne of St Peter, a marble seat decorated with Moorish motifs and Koranic inscriptions, cut from an Arab *stele*. The patriarchal palace, converted into barracks by Napoleon, stands on the grassy *campo* alongside a tilting Renaissance belltower by Coducci.

Above: *San Michele's dome* ***Right:*** *San Pietro di Castello*

San Rocco

The grandest of the *scuole* or charitable lay confraternities, this society is dedicated to St Roch, the French saint of plague victims, who so impressed the Venetians that they stole his relics and canonised him. Their mission to relieve the sick soon became conflated with the prestige and social standing of the *scuola*.

A pictorial cycle of Tintoretto adorns the walls of the 16th-century building. In the evening, this splendid stage acts as a backdrop for baroque recitals. The painter's overpowering Biblical scenes provoke strong responses. Henry James found "the air thick with genius" yet palpably human: "It is not immortality that we breathe at San Rocco but conscious, reluctant mortality".

Stagily set on easels by the altar are several great paintings, notably Tiepolo's *Abraham and the Angels* and Titian's poetic *Annunciation*, matched by his *Christ Carrying the Cross*. The Sala dell'Albergo contains allegories linked to the society's patron saint, including *St Roch in Glory*, the ceiling panel that won Tintoretto the entire commission. The *Crucifixion* faces it: both a vast masterpiece with a charged atmosphere and a poignant drama.

Scuola Grande di San Rocco

Once the richest Venetian confraternities, this *scuola* proves the exception to the rule that Venetian interiors are finer than exteriors. The confraternity retains its *trompe l'oeil* Renaissance facade as well as its assembly rooms and chapterhouse. Coducci designed the curved crowning of the facade in 1490. The Lombardi brothers decorated the sumptuous marble lower section.

A grand portal framed by illusionistic lions leads into the hushed city hospital, with the foyer occupying the cloisters of the former Dominican foundation. To visit the former *scuola* walk upstairs to check the current opening times posted on the door of the medical library, housed in the panelled, 16th-century assembly rooms.

Torcello Island

The long boat trip to Torcello helps one appreciate the remoteness of this evocative island, the earliest centre of Venetian

Above: *Scuola Grande di San Rocco facade detail*

civilisation. The austerely lovely basilica of Santa Fosca, built by Greeks, is a *martyrium*, housing the relics of a martyr. This coherent masterpiece, harmoniously combines Romanesque and Byzantine elements. Santa Maria dell'Assunta, a model of an early Christian church is the oldest monument in the lagoon: founded in 639 as an episcopal seat.

San Zaccaria

This delightful church is graced by Coducci's curvilinear facade. It conceals a far older basilica, with Byzantine and Gothic churches fused into a harmonious Renaissance whole. The church was founded in the 9th century and acted as a Venetian pantheon, with eight early Doges buried in the crypt. The original Byzantine basilica forms the crypt below San Tarasio chapel.

The Zattere

The Zattere stretches all the way round Dorsoduro's southern shore. This promenade, created in 1516 and named after the cargoes of wood that were unloaded on these quaysides *(zattere* means "floating rafts") makes a refreshing *fondamente* and the Venetians' favourite walking place.

In all seasons, strolling along the Zattere represents a local ritual. At the first sign of spring sunshine, Venetian sun-worshippers flock to the landing stages and decks that line the shore.

Above: *the Zattere promenade*

ESSENTIAL INFORMATION

The Place

The Venetian lagoon covers over 500 sq km (193 sq miles), which is roughly divided – biologically speaking – between "dead" and "living" lagoons. Venice itself comprises 118 islands, 45 km (28 miles) of canals and 400 bridges.
Population: Approximately 320,000.
Language: Italian (and Venetian dialect).
Religion: Roman Catholic.
Time Zone: Central European Time (GMT plus one hour).
Currency: Italian lira; switching to the euro in 2002.
Weights and Measures: Metric.
Electricity: 220 volts. You will need an adaptor to operate British three-pin appliances and a transformer for 100–120 volt appliances.
International Dialling Code: From the UK, dial 00 39 41 plus the number you require. From within Italy, including from within Venice itself, dial 041 plus the number.

Climate

The Venetian climate is notoriously capricious, with a whole spectrum of different weather possible in one day, particularly in spring and winter. January can be bitterly cold, wet and windy and then suddenly illuminated by warm sunshine.

Humidity affects the hottest and coldest days. Venice in the height of summer can be oppressively muggy. The most rain generally falls in March to April and November to December. *Acqua alta*, the condition Venetians loathe, occurs between autumn and spring. It includes exceptionally high tides flooding the low-

Left: *the ubiquitous gondolas*

lying areas of the city (San Marco is often included). The city is exposed to frequent fogs and two harsh winds: the *bora* blows from the Steppes in winter and the *scirocco* brings hot weather from the Middle East. That said, Venice experiences sunny days and limpid light over the lagoon in all seasons, but the loveliest months of the year are probably May, June and September. The average temperatures are: January 3.8°C (38.8°F); April 12.6°C (54.6°F); July 23.6°C (74.4°F); and October 15.1°C (59.1°F).

Government

Venice is the capital of the Veneto, the wealthy region in north-eastern Italy that has one of the highest per capita incomes in Italy. In administrative terms, Venice and the mainland communities come under the same local government. The city mayor wields considerable power. However, factional in-fighting between the two communities of mainland Venice and historic Venice means that the city is likely to experience continuing turmoil.

Economy

Venice is heavily dependent on tourism, including such sectors as independent, package and conference tourism as well as glass-making, lace- and mask-making, restoration and antiques dealing. Tourism and the craft industry are supplemented by the declining sectors of fishing, boat-building and market-gardening.

Above: *a street sign clear in any language*

Public Holidays

1 January New Year's Day; **6 January** Epiphany; **March/April** Easter Monday; **25 April** Liberation Day; **1 May** May Day; **15 August** August holiday; **1 November** All Saints; **8 December** Immaculate Conception; **25 December** Christmas Day; **26 December** Boxing Day.

Getting There

BY AIR

The main airport is Marco Polo, 13 km (8 miles) from the city centre. However, some charter companies confusingly refer to Treviso airport as "Venice airport". This is, in fact, 30 km (19 miles) to the north of Venice and far less convenient, so check which airport your travel agent is offering you. Alitalia is the main agent for flights to Venice. Domestically direct flights serve Naples, Rome and Palermo to Venice.

Several UK airports offer direct scheduled and charter flights: Apex British Airways (020 8897 4000), Go (tel: 0845-6054321), Ryanair (08701-569569), as well as summer charters from Gatwick, Manchester and Birmingham.

From North America, the majority of flights to Venice stop over in either London, Frankfurt, Amsterdam, Rome or Milan.

Right: *a mime artist in bright costume*

BY CAR

Costs of travelling to Venice by car include petrol, motorway tolls, hotels en route and the car park fees in Venice. You will need a current driving licence (with an Italian translation unless it is the standard EU licence) and valid insurance (green card). However, arriving by car is generally best avoided since it must be left in a car park outside Venice.

BY TRAIN

International services arrive from London (changing in Paris), Moscow, Munich, Nice, Paris, Vienna, St Petersburg and Zurich. Train fares often match those of flying. However, the advantages of travelling by train include the chance to see some of Europe's most beautiful landscapes and make stops along the way. Within Italy, trains connect Venice from Bologna, Genoa, Ferrara, Milan, Turin and Verona. If travelling from Rome, the high-speed Pendolino service offers a quicker service with higher prices.

Above: *gondolas and canals are everywhere in the city*

Entry Regulations

For visits up to three months, visas are not required by visitors from EU countries, the US, Canada, Australia or New Zealand. A valid passport (or in the case of those from EU member countries, a valid identification card) is sufficient. Nationals of most other countries require a visa. This must be obtained in advance from an Italian Embassy.

Money

Venice is the most expensive city in Italy. Until the euro conversion in 2002, the unit of currency will remain the lira. There are 1,000, 2,000, 5,000, 10,000, 50,000 and 100,000 lire bills and 100, 200 and 500 lire coins. Travellers' cheques are the safest way to carry money, and American Express and Thomas Cook the most recognised in Italy. Many hotels do not accept travellers' cheques but larger stores probably will. Most large shops and restaurants in Venice accept major credit cards, but they are used less in Italy than in North America or Northern Europe.

Banks open from Monday–Friday 8.30am– 1.30pm and some open in the afternoon from 2.30–3.30pm or from 3.30–4.30pm. You will need to have your passport or identification card with you when changing money. Remember changing money is a slow operation in Italy. Regular customers will tend to be served before you, so allow plenty of time and, ideally, visit in the morning.

Above: *the train gives you the chance to see some great countryside*

Accommodation

Venetian hotel rates are the third highest in the world, after Hong Kong and Moscow, and 10 and 30 percent higher than the Italian mainland. Booking a package with a reputable Italian specialist usually provides some respite from Venice's high rates. Demand exceeds supply during the main tourist season (April–September) so it's wise to book early.

Venetian hoteliers often boast their city has no off-season. Certainly, city hotels are heavily booked during the Venetian Carnival in February, Christmas and New Year. In November, January and March, many of the hotels on the Lido and certain grand hotels close. However, room rates in some hotels fall during this period. During the summer, many Venetian hotels, especially those on the Lido, may insist on a half- or full-board arrangement.

Many hotels in Venice deserve a visit in their own right. The Danieli (arguably Venice's most historic hotel) even enchanted Proust: "When I went to Venice I found that my dream had become – incredibly but quite simply – my address". Next door the charming Londra Palace boasts "a hundred windows on the lagoon". In splendid rooms overlooking San Giorgio, Tchaikovsky composed his Fourth Symphony.

The Luna Baglioni claims to be the oldest hotel in Venice dating back to Templar time, and Gritti Palace hosted such artists as Ruskin, Hemingway and Graham Greene.

***Above:** capturing the moment*

Getting Around

BY CAR

Visitors arriving by car will need to leave it at one of several car parks at the entrance to the city. The multi-storey car park at Piazzale Roma is close to the centre and has good ferry services but is expensive. By contrast, the island of Tronchetto (built on reclaimed land) forms the largest car park in Europe and, although cheaper, is further away from the centre and less accessible by ferry. You may have to wait for half an hour or so for a ferry. Prices vary considerably at both car parks, depending on the car and the season, but 30,000 lire per day is an absolute minimum. Queues can be extremely long at the height of summer. Ferry line 82 links Tronchetto with central Venice.

WATER TRANSPORT

City ferries or water buses are usually known as *vaporetti*. When you arrive in Venice, it is worth buying a one- or three-day or weekly travel pass, which will allow you to travel on any city ferry, including to the islands (boats to the airport are excluded). Travel passes are relatively expensive but are cheaper and less fuss than buying individual trips. If you are found without a ticket, a fine is payable on the spot. The pass can be bought in

***Right:** a typical way to travel in watery Venice*

Piazzale Roma and at San Zaccaria, among other places. There are also passes for family or friends, although you need to be in a group of three or more. It is worth picking up the current transport map from the office at Piazzale Roma or collecting a copy of the invaluable booklet *Un Ospite a Venezia/A Guest in Venice* (in Italian and English) from any of the grand hotels.

The most confusing landing stages are at San Zaccaria (on Riva degli Schiavoni), San Marco and Fondamente Nuove, because they are spread out along the quaysides, with different services running from different jetties.

One of the easiest mistakes is to travel in the wrong direction, especially if it's dark and you can't see any landmarks. Ferries are usually designated as being *circolare a destra* or *circolare a sinistra*; these do the same route in both directions. Ask one of the boatmen as you board: "*Va bene per San Marco/Il Lido/Torcello?*" (Is this right for San Marco/the Lido/Torcello? etc.). Ferries with barred numbers do not necessarily operate the same route as the unbarred ferry of the same number: it is often a truncated or restricted route.

Except during such events as the Film Festival and

Above: *Murano police boat*

the Biennale, water taxis are readily available. There are taxi stands at Piazzale Roma; Santa Lucia railway station (Ferrovia); at the Rialto; San Marco; on the Lido; and at Marco Polo airport. This is a stylish but prohibitively expensive option for visitors. Even though there are official rates from the airport to the city centre, and from the city centre to the main islands, it is tricky to get many water taxis to agree to them. Certainly, try and agree a price before setting out to your destination.

However, if the taxi is dropping you off outside the city centre and returning to the centre empty, you will probably have to pay this fare or his hourly rate. In addition, there are numerous extra charges, including a call-out charge, a charge per person, a baggage charge and a nightly rate.

The city has a number of gondola stands, indicated by the word "stazio" on a map. The biggest official stands are at Bacino Orseolo, behind St Mark's; at Calle Vallaresso, west of St Mark's; and on the Molo, in front of the Doge's Palace. More stands are scattered throughout the city and are readily visible. A good place for watching gondolas is from the cafe overlooking the canal on Campo Santa Maria Formosa; there is a gondola stand beside it.

You must agree on a price with the gondolier before starting. Music or singing is always extra but first agree a price (not all gondoliers sing or play music but they can organise it quickly with a colleague). Although this service can be derided as hackneyed, it is often surprisingly good.

Above: *a novel take on the gondola*

Festivals

La Festa di San Marco, held on 25 April honours the city's patron saint. Marco Cè. The Patriarch of Venice ushers in the occasion with solemn celebrations at San Marco and greets dignitaries in the Cappella di San Teodoro. Tradition states that sweethearts receive a rosebud, *il bocolo*, on this day. Girls take any rosebud tokens of love and place them on Saint Mark's grave.

La Sensa, held the Sunday after Ascension Day, celebrates Venice's Marriage with the Sea.

La Vogalonga, an endurance race on the Sunday following La Sensa. Oar-powered craft take part in a marathon regatta.

La Festa del Redentore, the most romantic and intimate of Venetian festivals takes place on the third Sunday of July. The festival focuses on *Il Redentore*, the Palladian church built on Giudecca as a token of thanks after salvation from the plague of 1576. A sweeping bridge of boats stretches across the Giudecca canal to the church, enabling people to attend Mass and listen to the chanting monks.

La Regata Storica, the Historical Regatta, held on the first Sunday in September features participants in Renaissance costume.

La Festa della Madonna della Salute, on 21 November, commemorates the city's deliverance from the plague of 1630. Venetians make the pilgrimage to La Salute to light candles in thanks for the continuing good health of the city and its citizens.

Above: *gondoliers plying the waters of Venice*

Tourist Offices Abroad

ENIT **Canada**, 17 Bloor Street East, Suite 907-South Tower, M4W 3R Toronto, Ontario, tel: 416-925 4882.

ENIT **UK**, 1 Princes Street, London W1R 8AY, tel: 020-7355 1557.

ENIT **United States**, 630 5th Avenue, Suite 565, New York, NY 10111, tel: 212-245 4822; 500 N Michigan Avenue, Suite 2240, Chicago, IL 60611, tel: 312-644 0990; 12400 Wilshire Blvd, Ste 550, Los Angeles, CA 90025, tel: 310- 820 1898.

Websites

www.elmoro.com a virtual Venice, extensive maps, travel and transport information and online booking for selected hotels.

www.venicerentals.com apartments and houses for holiday rental

www.doge.it links to hotels online and current events listings.

www.veniceword.com news magazine.

www.carnivalofvenice.com official site of Venice's biggest event.

Above: *carnival dolls all in a row*

Language

Yes Si/**No** No

Thank you Grazie

You're welcome Prego

Alright/That's fine Va bene

Please Per favore or per cortesia

Excuse me (to get attention) Scusi (singular), Scusate (plural)

Excuse me (in a crowd) Permesso

Excuse me (to attract attention from, eg. a waiter) Senta!

Excuse me (sorry) Mi scusi

I don't know Non lo so

I don't understand Non capisco

Do you speak English/French Parla Inglese/Francese?

Could you speak more slowly Può parlare piu lentamente, per favore?

Could you repeat that please? Può ripetere, per piacere?

Yesterday/today/tomorrow ieri/oggi/domani

Now/early/late adesso/presto/tardi

What Quale/come?

When/why/where quando/perchè/dove?

Above: *looking towards San Maggiore*

And now for the big picture…

The text you have been reading is extracted from *Insight Guide: Venice*, one of more than 200 titles in the award-winning Insight Guides series. Its 350 pages are packed with expert essays covering Venice's history and culture, detailed itineraries for the city and the islands of the lagoon, comprehensive listings, a full set of cross-referenced maps, and hundreds of great photographs. It's an inspiring background read, an invaluable on-the-spot companion, and a superb souvenir of a visit. Available from all good bookshops.

INSIGHT GUIDES

The world's largest collection of visual travel guides